7 Daily Confessions

B. B. HICKS

WESTBOW
PRESS
A DIVISION OF THOMAS NELSON

The scripture quotations are taken from the Holy Bible, The Old & New Testments. Kings James Version. Super Giant Print Reference Bible. Broadman & Holman Publishers. Copyright 1996.

WestBow Press books may be ordered through booksellers or by contacting:

WestBow Press
A Division of Thomas Nelson
1663 Liberty Drive
Bloomington, IN 47403
www.westbowpress.com
1 (866) 928-1240

ISBN: 978-1-4908-1042-3 (sc)
ISBN: 978-1-4908-1041-6 (e)

Library of Congress Control Number: 2013917609

Printed in the United States of America.

WestBow Press rev. date: 09/25/2013

Dedication

This book is dedicated to my mother Florence Maiten, Pastor Leon Washington, Mother Mary L. Hall, the late Deacon Isaac Dawson, my best friend Kim R. Johnson, and most of all to my loving family; James, Sondra, Tiffany, Jordon, Tatiana, Todd and Jay. I thank all my friends and family for their love, support and assistance during this book's evolution.

Contents

Foreword

The word of God proclaims that we can have whatsoever we say if we doubt not in our hearts and is in right standing with God. These confessions focus on this point, as well as how we as heirs of God are entitled to certain benefits which are found in the word of the only true and living God. I enjoyed reading this book and believe that both men and women alike will benefit from reading and confessing the words of God.

Evangelist Mary L Hall
St. Marys, GA

Acknowledgements

A DECLARATION OF DEPENDENCE

I want to take this opportunity to thank God for His mercy, grace and for giving me the vision to write this book. Without His help it would not have been possible. I thank God who is my source, for His words, his leading and guidance throughout this journey. I thank Him for the thoughts and ideas that he has given me to relay to his people. Additionally, I want to thank and acknowledge all my spiritual leaders and teachers for sharing their faith, time and knowledge.

Introduction

7 DAILY CONFESSIONS

According to the scriptures, we, as saints, can have whatsoever we say, if we doubt not in our hearts and believe that those things which we have said shall come to pass.

The 7 Daily Confessions was written with this premise in mind and with the intention to bring about a positive change in the lives of believers by confessing the true and living word of God. This concept calls for a paradigm shift in the body of Christ in order to empower the saints to SPEAK THE WORD ONLY and speak those things that be not as though they were, while knowing that manifestation is just a matter of time. In faith we have to believe that we receive from God, at the time of our asking, and we are to wait patiently for the manifestation of the desired result. While we are waiting for the manifestation we are to concurrently let our actions and our spoken words and thoughts line up with the word of God. We can cancel our prayers and confession by wrong thinking and speaking doubt and unbelief. So we must stand strong and stay in faith and continue to trust God's word. We must have the mindset about God that says; even if he don't, I know my God is able. So, let us now, start speaking God's word and standing on his promises. Staying in faith, never doubting, just believing God's word is true. Our believing and our confessing must line up with God's word. The bible tells us that God's words will not return to him void and that he watches over his word to perform it (Isaiah 55:11). These 7 confessions are to be spoken aloud and declared daily and our expectations must remain strong. In Genesis we see how God's spoken words brought everything into existence and we who are made in his image and likeness possess the same capabilities by faith. This is a faith book that is based solely on the belief in the words of God; such as in the power of the tongue, and in the calling of those things that be not as though they were (Hebrews 11) and in the fact that expectation never leads to failure. So start speaking, declaring, decreeing, and confessing God's word, and wait by faith for the manifestation of the desired results (Hebrews 11:1).

And Jesus answering saith unto them, Have faith in God, For verily I say unto you, That whosoever shall say unto this mountain, Be thou removed, and be thou cast into the sea; and shall not doubt in his heart, but shall believe that those things which he saith shall come to pass; he shall have whatsoever he saith.

Mark 11:22-23

DAY 1

A Declaration of Blessing

Daily Confession

DAY 1
A DECLARATION OF BLESSING

Lord, I thank you for this day and for allowing me to see another day. I confess that I am a child of the Most High God. I am blessed of the Lord and anointed to do his will. I am blessed in my going out and in my coming in (Deut. 28:6). Father, in the name of Jesus, enlarge my territory, I ask that you bless me indeed (1 Chronicles 4:10). I know that I am blessed in order to be a blessing unto others, so Lord, help me to give unselfishly to those who are in need, as you direct me in my giving. Lord, you have satisfied my mouth with good things, so that my youth is renewed like the eagle (Psalms 103:5). Lord, your word says that if I don't let your book of the law depart out of my mouth and if I meditate therein day and night, and do according to all that is written therein then my way will be prosperous and I will have good success (Josh 1:8). I decree in the name of Jesus, that I can do all things through Christ Jesus who strengthen me (Phil. 4:13), and it is my desire to do your will. Greater is he that is in me, than he that is in this world (1 John 4:4). Lord, I thank you for making me the head and not the tail and above only and not beneath (Deut. 28:13). I love my father who is in heaven, because he first loved me. There is no greater love than what you have for me because while I was yet a sinner you sent your son to die for me, so that I might have life and to have it more abundantly (John 3:16, John 10:10). According to God's word all things are working together for my good, and my God shall supply all of my needs according to his riches and glory by Christ Jesus (Romans 8:28, Phil. 4:19). For the word says that in the Lord's house there are many mansions and he is rich and owns cattle on a thousand hills (John 14:2, Psalms 50:10). I am blessed of the Lord, because God has cleansed me from all unrighteousness, and now I am like a good tree that bringeth forth good fruits (Matt 7:17).

Daily Confession

DAY 1
SCRIPTURES
A DECLARATION OF BLESSING

Deuteronomy 28:6—Blessed shalt thou be when thou comest in, and blessed shalt thou be when thou goest out. (KJV)

1 Chronicles 4:10—And Jabez called on the God of Israel, saying, Oh that thou wouldest bless me indeed, and enlarge my coast, and that thine hand might be with me, and that thou wouldest keep me from evil, and that it may not grieve me! And God granted him that which he requested. (KJV)

Psalms 103:5—Who satisfieth they mouth with good things; so that thy youth is renewed like the eagle's. (KJV)

Joshua 1:8—This book of the law shall not depart out of thy mouth; but thou shalt mediate therein day and night, that thou mayest observe to do according to all that is written therein: for then thou shalt make thy way prosperous, and then thou shalt have good success. (KJV)

Philippians 4:13—I can do all things through Christ which strengtheneth me. (KJV)

1 John 4:4—Ye are of God, little children, and have overcome them: because greater is he that is in you, than he that is in the world. (KJV)

Deuteronomy 28:13—And the Lord shall make thee the head, and not the tail; and thou shalt be above only, and thou shalt not be beneath; if that thou hearken unto the commandments of the Lord they God, which I command thee this day, to observe and to do them: (KJV)

John 3:16—For God so loved the world, that he gave his only begotten Son, that whosoever believeth in him should not perish, but have everlasting life. (KJV)

John 10:10—The thief cometh not, but for to steal, and to kill and to destroy: I am come that they might have life, and that they might have it more abundantly. (KJV)

Romans 8:28—And we know that all things work together for good to them that love God, to them who are called according to his purpose. (KJV)

Philippians 4:19—But my God shall supply all your need according to his riches in glory by Christ Jesus. (KJV)

John 14:2—In my Father's house are many mansions: if it were not so, I would have told you. I go to prepare a place for you. (KJV)

Psalms 50:10—For every beast of the forest is mine, and the cattle upon a thousand hills. (KJV)

Matthew 7:17—Even so every good tree bringeth forth good fruit; but a corrupt tree bringeth forth evil fruit. (KJV)

Day 2

A Declaration of Protection

Daily Confession

DAY 2

A DECLARATION OF PROTECTION

Today I declare that I will abide under the shadow of the Most High God (Psalms 91:1). The Lord is my light and my salvation whom shall I fear? The Lord is the strength of my life of whom shall I be afraid (Psalms 27:1)? The Lord did not give me the spirit of fear but of power, love and a sound mind (Romans 8:15). Lord, I thank you for the power, love and the soundness of mind that you have given me. Thank you, Father, for your mercy and grace and for watching over me each and every day. Lord, I thank you for the hedge of protection that you have placed around me. I declare in the name of Jesus, that I am a mighty warrior of God and his angels are encamped around me. In the name of Jesus, I put on the whole Armor of God. I put on the helmet of salvation, the breastplate of righteousness, I gird my loin in truth, I shod my feet with the preparation of the gospel of peace, and most of all, I take up shield of faith and the sword of the spirit, which is the word of God (Ephesians 6:10-17). Finally, Father as I stand this day, fully suited in your armor, I am like a tree planted by the rivers of water that bring forth his fruit in his season; my leaf also shall not wither; and whatsoever I do shall prosper (Psalms 1:3).

Daily Confession

DAY 2
SCRIPTURES
A DECLARATION OF PROTECTION

Psalms 91:1—He that dwelleth in the secret place of the most High shall abide under the shadow of the Almighty. (KJV)

Psalms 27:1—The Lord is my light and my salvation; whom shall I fear? The Lord is the strength of my life; of whom shall I be afraid? (KJV)

Romans 8:15—For ye have not received the spirit of bondage again to fear, but ye have received the Spirit of adoption, whereby we cry, Abba, Father. (KJV)

Ephesians 6:10-17—(10) Finally, my brethren, be strong in the Lord, and in the power of his might. (11) Put on the whole armour of God, that ye may be able to stand against the wiles of the devil. (12) For we wrestle not against flesh and blood, but against principalities, against powers, against rulers of the darkness of this world, against spiritual wickedness in high places. (13) Wherefore take unto you the whole armour of God, that ye may be able to withstand in the evil day, and having done all, to stand. (14) Stand therefore, having your loins girt about with truth, and having on the breastplate of righteousness; (15) And your feet shod with the preparation of the gospel of peace; (16) Above all, taking the shield of faith, wherewith ye shall be able to quench all the fiery darts of wicked. (17) And take the helmet of salvation, and the sword of the Spirit, which is the word of God: (KJV)

Psalms 1:3—And he shall be like a tree planted by the rivers of water, that bringeth forth his fruit in his season, his leaf also shall not wither; and whatsoever he doeth shall prosper. (KJV)

DAY 3

A Declaration of Praise

Daily Confession

DAY 3
A DECLARATION OF PRAISE

I will make a joyful noise unto the Lord. I will serve the Lord with gladness and come before his presence with singing. For it is he who has made us, and not we ourselves; we are his people, the sheep of his pasture. I will enter his gates with thanksgiving and into his courts with praise. I will be thankful unto the Lord and bless his holy name. For the Lord is good; his mercy is everlasting; and his truth endureth to all generations (Psalms 100). O taste and see that the Lord is good: blessed is the man that trusteth in him (Psalms 34:8). Dear Father in Heaven, I submit unto you an attitude of constant praise, for I know you inhabit the praise of your people (Psalms 22:3). Father, I decree that you are the Lord of lords, and King of kings and worthy to be praised. You are Lord of my life. You are an awesome God and worthy to be praised. So, I praise you in spirit and in truth. I thank you for your mercy and grace that is renewed day by day. Lord without you I could do nothing, without you in my life, I would fail. Lord, I thank you for filling me with your precious Holy Spirit, because he leads and directs my steps (John 14:16). All I am, I owe to you, because you are the author and finisher of my faith (Hebrews 12:2). Lord, today I give you all honor, all the glory, and all the praise, for you alone is worthy and deserving of it all. So, let everything that hath breath praise the Lord, Praise ye the Lord (Psalms 150:6).

Daily Confession

Day 3
Scriptures
A Declaration of Praise

Psalms 100—(1) Make a joyful noise unto the Lord, all ye lands. (2) Serve the Lord with gladness: come before his presence with singing. (3) Know ye that the Lord he is God: it is he that hath made us, and not we ourselves; we are his people, and the sheep of his pasture. (4) Enter into his gates with thanksgiving, and into his courts with praise: be thankful unto him, and bless his name. (5) For the Lord is good; his mercy is everlasting; and his truth endureth to all generations. (KJV)

Psalms 34:8—O taste and see that the Lord is good: blessed is the man that trusteth in him. (KJV)

Psalms 22:3—But thou art holy, O thou that inhabitest the praises of Israel. (KJV)

John 14:16—And I will pray the Father, and he shall give you another Comforter, that he may abide with you for ever, (KJV)

19

Hebrews 12:2—Looking unto Jesus the author and finisher of our faith; who for the joy that was set before him endured the cross, despising the shame, and is set down at the right hand of the throne of God. (KJV)

Psalms 150:6—Let every thing that hath breath praise the Lord. Praise ye the Lord. (KJV)

DAY 4

A Declaration of Joy

Daily Confession

DAY 4
A DECLARATION OF JOY

I will make a joyful noise unto the Lord, I will sing forth the honor of his name, and will make his praise glorious (Psalms 66:1-2). This is the day that the Lord hath made, and I will rejoice and be glad in it (Psalms 118:24). I know that weeping may endure for the night but my joy will come in the morning (Psalms 30:5). I am strong in the Lord because the joy of the Lord is my strength (Nehemiah 8:10). I thank you God, for you are my strength and my redeemer. Lord your word says I am to count it all joy even when I fall into divers temptations knowing that the trying of my faith worketh patient, and letting patient have her perfect work in me so that I may be perfect and entire wanting nothing (James 1:2-4). Father, in the name of Jesus, I ask this day, for your joy, peace, guidance and protection to abide with me all the day long. Father, teach me to be content in all situations (Philippians 4:11-12). Father there is no greater love than what you have for me because while I was yet a sinner, you sent your son to die for me (John 3:16, John 15:13), so that I may have life and have it more abundantly (John 10:10). Lord you are my Shepherd, and I shall not follow any other and I shall not want for anything. You maketh me to lie down in green pastures; and leadeth me beside the still waters (Psalms 23:1-2). Father I know you are a rewarder of them that diligently seek you (Hebrews 11:6), and I will seek you daily and will find you. For according to your word, those that seek shall find, knock and it shall be open, ask and it shall be given (Matt. 7:7, Luke 11:9). I rejoice because my name is written in heaven (Luke 10:20) in the Lamb's book of life (Rev 21:2).

Daily Confession

DAY 4
SCRIPTURES
A DECLARATION OF JOY

Psalms 66:1-2—(1) Make a joyful noise unto God, all ye lands: (2) Sing forth the honour of his name: make his praise glorious. (KJV)

Psalms 118:24—This is the day which the Lord hath made, we will rejoice and be glad in it. (KJV)

Psalms 30:5—For his anger endureth but a moment, in his favours is life: weeping may endure for a night, but joy cometh in the morning. (KJV)

Nehemiah 8:10—Then he said unto them, Go your way, eat the fat, and drink the sweet, and send portions unto them for whom nothing is prepared: for this day is holy unto our Lord: neither be ye sorry; for the joy of the Lord is your strength. (KJV)

James 1:2-4—(2) My brethren, count it all joy when ye fall into divers temptations; (3)

Knowing this, that the trying of your faith worketh patience. (4) But let patience have her perfect work, that ye may be perfect and entire, wanting nothing. (KJV)

Philippians 4:11-12—(11) Not that I speak in respect of want: for I have learned, in whatsoever state I am, therewith to be content. (12) I know both how to be abased, and I know how to abound: every where and in all things I am instructed both to be full and to be hungry, both to abound and to suffer need. (KJV)

John 3:16—For God so loved the world, that he gave his only begotten Son, that whosoever believeth in him should not perish, but have everlasting life. (KJV)

John 15:13—Greater love hath no man than this, that a man lay down his life for his friends. (KJV)

John 10:10—The thief cometh not, but for to steal, and to kill, and to destroy: I am come that they might have life, and that they might have it more abundantly. (KJV)

Psalms 23:1-2—(1) The Lord is my shepherd; I shall not want. (2) He maketh me to lie down in green pastures: he leadeth me beside the still waters. (KJV)

Hebrews 11:6—But without faith it is impossible to please him: for he that cometh to God must believe that he is, and that he is a rewarder of them that diligently seek him. (KJV)

Matthew 7:7—Ask, and it shall be given you; seek, and ye shall find; knock, and it shall be opened unto you: (KJV)

Luke 11:9—And I say unto you, Ask, and it shall be given, you; seek, and ye shall find; knock, and it shall be opened unto you. (KJV)

Luke 10:20—Notwithstanding in this rejoice not, that the spirits are subject unto you; but rather rejoice, because your names are written in heaven. (KJV)

Revelation 21:27—And there shall in no wise enter into it any thing that defileth, neither whatsoever worketh abomination, or maketh a lie: but they which are written in the Lamb's book of life.

DAY 5

A Declaration of Peace

Daily Confession

DAY 5
A DECLARATION OF PEACE

Lord, you are my peace. I cast all my cares upon you (1 Peter 5:7). According to your word I am to be careful for nothing; but in everything by prayer and supplication with thanksgiving to let my requests be made known unto you; and your peace which passeth all understanding, shall keep my heart and mind through Christ Jesus (Philippians 4:6-7). I thank Lord for keeping me, and for giving me your peace. Father, I am determined to go all the way with you, I am pressing on toward the mark of your high calling because of your grace and mercy (Philippians 3:14). I thank you for encasing me in your loving arms of protection. I will dwell in the secret place of the most High and abide under the shadow of the Almighty (Psalms 91:1). Father, as I decrease, may you increase in my life so that I may not walk after the flesh but after the spirit, and that I may worship you in spirit and in truth (John 4:24). I pray for all men, kings, and for all those who are in positions of authority so that I may lead a quiet and peaceable life in the land. (1Timothy

2:1-2). Lord thank you for sitting on the right hand of the Father making intercessions on my behalf (Romans 8:34). Lord, I acknowledge you this day as my Lord, my Savior, my God. I ask that you lead and direct my path (Proverbs 3:5-6). I want to be like David, the apple of your eye (Psalms 17:8), a person after your own heart (1 Samuel 13:14) having a pure heart and an upright spirit. Finally, Father, I know you will keep me in perfect peace, when my mind is stayed on you (Isaiah 26: 3).

Daily Confession

DAY 5
SCRIPTURES
A DECLARATION OF PEACE

1 Peter 5:7—Casting all your care upon him; for he careth for you.

Philippians 4:6-7—(6)Be careful for nothing; but in every thing by prayer and supplication with thanksgiving let your requests be made known unto God. (7)

And the peace of God, which passeth all understanding, shall keep your hearts and minds through Christ Jesus. (KJV)

Psalms 91:1—He that dwelleth in the secret place of the most High shall abide under the shadow of the Almighty. (KJV)

1Timothy 2:1-2—(1) I exhort therefore, that, first of all, supplications, prayers, intercessions, and giving of thanks, be made for all men; (2) For kings, and for all in authority, that we may lead a quiet and peaceable life in all godliness and honesty. (KJV)

Philippians 3:14—I press toward the mark for the prize of the high calling of God in Christ Jesus. (KJV)

Romans 8:34—Who is he that condemneth? It is Christ that died, yea rather, that is risen again, who is even at the right hand of God, who also maketh intercession for us. (KJV)

Proverbs 3:5-6—(5)Trust in the Lord with all thine heart; and lean not unto thine own understanding. (6) In all thy ways acknowledge him, and he shall direct thy paths. (KJV)

Psalms 17:8—Keep me as the apple of the eye, hid me under the show of thy wings, (KJV)

1 Samuel 13:14—But now thy kingdom shall not continue: the Lord hath sought him a man after his own heart, and the Lord hath commanded him to be caption over his people, because thou hast not kept that which the Lord commanded thee. (KJV)

John 4:24—God is a Spirit: and they that worship him must worship him in spirit and in truth. (KJV)

Isaiah 26: 3—Thou wilt keep him in perfect peace, whose mind is stayed on thee; because he trusteth in thee. (KJV)

DAY 6

A Declaration of Faith

Daily Confession

DAY 6
A DECLARATION OF FAITH

Dear father in heaven, according to your word faith is the substance of things hoped for, the evidence of things not seen (Hebrews 11:1), and I know that faith cometh by hearing, and hearing by the word of God (Romans 10:17). God's word is true and is forever settled in heaven (Psalm 119:89). For God is not a man, that he should lie; neither the son of man, that he should repent: hath he said, and shall he not do it? Or hath he spoke and shall he not make it good (Numbers 23:19). God's words will not return to him void and that He watches over His word to perform it (Isaiah 55:11). Without faith, it is impossible to please God, and he that cometh to God must first believer that he is, and that he is a rewarder of them that diligently seek him (Hebrews 11:6). So, father I thank you for the measure of faith that you have given me (Romans12:3), for the word of faith is near me, in my mouth and in my heart (Romans 10:8). Out of the abundance of the heart the mouth speaketh (Matt 12:34). God you are my deliver, my strong tower, the source of my strength, my comforter, my healer, my God in whom I will trust. For your word tells us that we are to walk by faith and not by sight (2 Cor 5:7) No matter what the situation may look like, I will trust God for my help and strength because he is my God. He is all that his word says that he is, so I will be still and know that you are God. My God is omnipresent, omnipotent, and omniscient and because he is everywhere, all knowing, all powerful, and all knowing, I ask for His will to be done in my life, in the life of my family, my friends, and even in the life of my enemies. Additionally, Lord, let your will be done on earth, as it is in heaven. Father, I need you this day, and every day to lead and direct my steps. I am leaning and depending on you, for guidance, because without you I can do nothing but with God all things are possible (Matt 19:26) All I am, I owe to you because you are the author and finisher of my faith (Heb 12:2).

Daily Confession

DAY 6
SCRIPTURES
A DECLARATION OF FAITH

Hebrews 11:1—Now faith is the substance of things hoped for, the evidence of things not seen. (KJV)

Romans 10:17—So then faith cometh by hearing, and hearing by the word of God. (KJV)

Psalm 119:89—For ever, O Lord, thy word is settled in heaven.

Numbers 23:19—God is not a man, that he should lie; neither the son of man, that he should repent: hath he said, and shall he not do it? Or hath he spoken, and shall he not make it good? (KJV)

Isaiah 55:11—So shall my word be that goeth forth out of my mouth: it shall not return unto me void, but it shall accomplish that which I please, and it shall prosper in the thing whereto I sent it. (KJV)

Hebrews 11:6—But without faith it is impossible to please him; for he that cometh to God must believer that he is, and that he is a rewarder of them that diligently seek him. (KJV)

Romans12:3—For I say, through the grace given unto me, to every man that is among you, not to think of himself more highly than he ought to think; but to think soberly, according as God hath dealt to every man the measure of faith. (KJV)

Romans 10:8—But what saith it? The word is nigh thee, even in thy mouth, and in thy heart: that is, the word of faith, which we preach; (KJV)

Matthew 12:34—O generation of vipers, how can ye, being evil, speak good things? For out of the abundance of the heart the mouth speaketh. (KJV)

2 Corinthians 5:7—For we walk by faith, and not by sight: (KJV)

Matthew 19:26—But Jesus beheld them, and said unto them, With men this is impossible; but with God all things are possible. (KJV)

Heb 12:2—Looking unto Jesus the author and finisher of our faith; who for the joy that was set before him endured the cross despising the same, and is set down at the right hand of the throne of God.

DAY 7

A Declaration of Healing

Daily Confession

DAY 7
A DECLARATION OF HEALING

Heal me, Oh Lord and I shall be healed, save me and I shall be saved; for thou art my praise (Jeremiah 17:14).

I shall live and not die to declare the works of the Lord (Psalms118:17).

According to your word you want us to prosper and be in health, even as our soul prospereth (3 John 1:2). So, I thank you for my healing. I know that if I delight myself also in the Lord; he will give me the desires of mine heart. (Psalms 37:4) Lord, I thank you for forgiving all mines iniquities and healing all mine diseases (Psalms 103:3).

Jesus Christ was wounded for my transgression, bruised for my iniquities, the chastisement of my peace was upon him and with his stripes I am healed (Isaiah 53:5).

Bless the Lord oh my soul and all that is within me, bless his holy name. Bless the Lord, oh my soul forget not all his benefits; who forgiveth all my iniquities who healeth all my diseases (Psalms 103:1-3). For you Lord satisfies my mouth with good *things; so that* my youth is renewed like the eagle's (Psalms 103:5). I thank you Lord for supplying all my needs according to your riches and glory (Phil 4:19). I thank you that I am the head and not the tail, above and not beneath (Deuteronomy 28:13). I thank you for health and strength. I thank you for being the shepherd of my life and under your leadership, I know I shall not want for any good thing (Psalms 23:1). Father, I thank you for my healing, for your love, and for the blood of Jesus Christ. I thank you for my salvation; the gift of eternal life. Father, I ask in Jesus name, to let my works, words, thoughts, and my life, be pleasing and acceptable in your sight. I am healed of the Lord.

Daily Confession

DAY 7
SCRIPTURES
A DECLARATION OF HEALING

Isaiah 53:5—But he was wounded for our transgressions, he was bruised for our iniquities: the chastisement of our peace was upon him; and with his stripes we are healed. (KJV)

Psalms 103:3—Who forgiveth all thine iniquities; who healeth all thy diseases; (KJV)

Psalms 118:17—I shall not die, but live, and declare the works of the Lord. (KJV)

Jeremiah 17:14—Heal me,. O Lord, and I shall be healed, save me, and I shall be saved: for thou art my praise. (KJV)

Psalms 103:1-3—(1) Bless the Lord, O my soul: and all that is within me, bless his holy name (2) Bless the Lord, O my soul, and forget not all his benefits: (3) Who forgiveth all thine iniquities; who healeth all thy diseases; (KJV)

3 John 1:2—Beloved, I wish above all things that thou mayest prosper and be in health, even as thy soul prospereth. (KJV)

Psalms 37:4—Delight thyself also in the Lord; and he shall give thee the desires of thine heart. (KJV)

Psalms 103:5—Who satisfieth thy mouth with good things; so that thy youth is renewed like th eagle's (KJV)

Philippians 4:19—But my God shall supply all your need according to is riches in glory by Christ Jesus. (KJV)

Deuteronomy 28:13—And the Lord shall make thee the head, and not the tail; and thou shalt be above only, and thou shalt not be beneath; if that thou hearken unto the commandments of the Lord thy God, which I command thee this day, to observe and to do them: (KJV)

Psalms 23:1—The Lord is my shepherd; I shall not want. (KJV)

The Greatest Confession

If you are lost and don't know Jesus Christ as your Lord and Savior but want to know him; please read the confession on the following page. The bible tells us the God so loved the world that he gave his only begotten Son so that whosoever believe in him should not perish but have eternal life (John 3:16). According to God's word, if we confess with our mouth the Lord Jesus Christ, and shall believe in our hearts that God hath raised him from the dead then we shall be saved. (Romans 10:9).

Confession of Salvation

Father, I confess that I am a sinner, and I repent from all my sins. I ask you to forgive me for all my sins and to cleanse me from all unrighteousness. Lord, I ask you to come into my heart and be my Lord and Savior. I confess that you are Lord and the only true and living God. I confess with my mouth and I believe in my heart that Jesus died on the cross and rose again and because of your love for me and of the blood of Jesus Christ, I am now free from a life of sin and death. Jesus is the only way, the truth and the light. No one can come unto the Father except they come by Jesus Christ, my Lord and Savior (John 14:6). Lord, thank you for saving me. Lord, your word says we have all sinned and fallen short of the glory of the God and I know that since I have confessed my sins you are faithful and just to forgive me of all my sins and to cleanse me from all unrighteousness (1John 1:9). So, there is therefore now, after the cleansing of the blood, no condemnation, because I am now a new creature in Christ Jesus (Romans 8:1). Dear Father in Heaven, thank you Lord for creating a pure heart within me and for renewing a right spirit within me (Psalms 51:10). I once was lost but now I'm found, was blind but now I see. Amen

About the Author

B. B. Hicks is a native of Lamont, Mississippi. She is the daughter of the late Evangelist Florence Maiten and granddaughter of the late Pastor Daniel Walter Maiten. She is the wife of James Hicks for the past 33 years and mother of Sondra Graham and Tiffany Lattany. She has two loving grandchildren; Jordon M. Lattany and Tatiana A. Graham.

She attended Brunswick College and received her Associate's Degree in Nursing and later attended Brenau University and received her Bachelor's Degree in Nursing. She is a member of Evergreen Missionary Baptist Church, in Kingsland, GA, where Dr. Leon Washington is Pastor. She was baptized at age 6, grew up in the church and rededicated her life to Christ in June 2004. She is saved, loves the Lord, and is a woman who studies God's word.